AHLUMBA HARRIS

INSPIRED 2 PROSPER

AHLUMBA HARRIS

Inspired2Prosper

It's Never too Late to Turn a Dream or an I Wish into a Reality…

Ahlumba Harris

Copyright © 2012 Ahlumba Harris

Edited by: Yetmon Wright, WM Bradley

All rights reserved. No part of this book may be reproduced or transmitted for commercial or non commercial use in any form by any means, electronic or mechanical, including photocopying, recording, or by any information storage and retrieval system without written approval from the Author.

All Scripture references comes from The King James Version Bible

Library of Congress Control Number: 2012903903

ISBN-10: 978-061582336X
ISBN-13: 978-0615823362

To order additional copies of this book, contact:

Inspired2Prosper International LLC
contactus@inspired2prosper.com
www.ahlumba.com
www.inspired2prosper.com

DEDICATION

To the two loves of my life Aniyla Harris and Wesley Bradley. I love you both with all my heart.

CONTENTS

	Acknowledgments	i
1	Why Me?	1
2	Picking Up The Pieces	11
3	Will This Define Me?	18
4	How I Overcame…	25
5	You Can Too!	38
6	Author's Afterthought	46
7	Something Extra	49
8	Share Your Story	58

ACKNOWLEDGMENTS

If it had not been for the Lord that was on my side I would not be here today. For that reason and much more I give all honor, glory, and praise to my Lord and Savior Jesus Christ. Who unlike man who judged my outer appearance, God saw my heart and knew that there was much more to me then what was before me.

Aniyla, my precious daughter many a day my struggle became your own yet you never complained about what you did not have, but was always thankful for what was given to you. Though you have many of my traits I always thanked God that you did not have the negative ones for there is a kindness in you that I had to grow in with wisdom. You are my heart and out of my sin I was given a blessing…I love you mommy

Wesley, our journey together has not always been an easy one, but through it all you have always been a true friend and I thank God that he intertwined our paths.

My parents Robert Harris and Barber Zeigler what can I say? No seriously what can I say? Just kidding, I love you both. Mommy thank God you were not uptight and holy when you met daddy or I probably would not be here today

I thank all my family for their support.. Mr. Bradley I thank you for everything you have done for me and Aniyla, we love you.

Chapter 1

WHY ME?

"Don't ask why me? Demand to know why not me...for without the journey there is no story"

As I stared out the window I wondered "Why me? Is this really happening again?" Fear gripped me, twisting my stomach in knots, as I stared at the vast array of past due notices. Utility due, daughters after school care due, car insurance due, and no food in the house, with the added bonus of the creditors of my past breathing down my back. With a heavy heart I prayed for the health of my daughter because I did the unthinkable. Yes, I canceled her medical insurance so that I could have the additional income (which left my daughter unprotected) to pay my bills. In that moment I could not help but realize that my life was like an album with four hit tracks titled: Struggle, Lack, Debt, and Hardship --with Struggle on constant repeat.

* * * * * *

The life I have led has not always been a pretty one. My childhood was enjoyable enough until I looked around and realized that my home was not like my friends. We did not always have electricity, the telephone was off more often than on, and at times we were without a place to lay our head leaving the car the only shelter to call home. My parents had seven children which caused us to learn early on to do without simple things that most took for granted such as; food, clothes, a bed to sleep on, television and more.

When I came of age and became more aware of my parents plight and struggles daily I worried and feared the possibility of seeing our things on the side of the road and for that reason I kept my head in books of fiction because my reality was nothing I wanted to be a part of. Books were my way of escape.

When I read those stories of romance and wealth, I did not have to face or think about the life I endured or the constant never ending struggle of my parents. However to my embarrassment though I was an avid reader, I was a mediocre student. It was no exaggeration to say that I absolutely hated school and could best be described with two words – "extremely lazy." For that reason in class and life I was always tipping the scales of failure.

Two weeks before the end of my senior year, I was ready to give up. So I dropped out of high school and moved in with my best friend and her family for a year. In the words of Optimums Prime "Big Mistake" sure I felt like I had the mom from hell, my parents were strict, allowed me no freedom, and caused me to miss my senior prom to name a few. However, in that year what I discovered surprised me. I learned that my family did not have it as bad as I thought.

Throughout my family's entire struggle my mother (who I now know was the glue) did her best with what she was given to keep all seven of her children together, clothed (even though she sometimes made them herself) and fed even if that meant going to a restaurant to ask for whatever could be spared. Living that long but short period with my best friend's family was different; I had to look out for myself, it was not what my friend led me to believe her life was.

About a year later and one month before my twentieth birthday, I moved in with my oldest sister Bahia and encountered a lot of firsts. Thanks to Bahia I was given my first job and with it came other first such as my first apartment, car, and responsibility. But, unfortunately I was not taught or prepared to handle the responsibility that came with adulthood. I lacked the preparation and knowledge it took to be responsible especially when it came to paying bills. There began my slow descent down the same path as my parents. Most of the time I paid everything late if I paid it at all; I knew I was wrong but the guilt I felt was not enough to make me change my bad spending habits. If anything, it just got worse.

By the age of 27 I had already lived In 9 different apartments but only completed the lease on two, moved back home twice to live with my parents, lived with two of my sisters, and cousin during separate occasions, owned two cars, defaulted on most of my bills, and made one bad decision after another. I was out of control! My lack of disciplined was like a drug that caused me to set aside all rational thought and throw every responsibility to the wind just to fulfill whatever want I had for that moment. Down that perilous road I continued until the last undisciplined choice I made cost me everything.

****

Has there ever been something that you knew you could not afford but pursued it anyway? There has for me, to my own detriment "Cottage at Hampton Apartment's." From the moment I saw the community I knew that I wanted to live there. Even after I discovered the monthly rent was way over my price range which should have stopped me, but it looked like home. I applied and was approved for a thirteen month lease (thanks to some creative cutting and pasting...i.e. lies) for the apartment.

The first month's rent I paid late and for the next five months it was a roller coaster ride. By the sixth month I felt like 'The Titanic' I was sinking quickly and knew I had to get out. Constantly I was behind on all my bills, always worrying, barely able to live while still trying to keep up appearances. Oh yes, I was faking it like I was making it even though I was up to my neck in debt. If it had not been for God and the people he used to bless me I do not know how I would have lasted as long as I did. I fell so far behind on everything that I decided that it would be more beneficial for me to cut my losses and just move somewhere more affordable.

Feeling good about my decision, I chose not to pay my last month of rent and instead I looked for a more affordable apartment. Normally that would be an easy task but not for me. My credit history was awful and the rental history was even worse. It was as if anyone who took a chance on me got stung. Finally, I was reaping what I sowed. Normally when trouble hit I would run just as I was trying to do then, yet every application I submitted was denied...nevertheless I could not give up because I had to get out before I received an eviction notice!

There I was on the verge of collapse and under extreme duress at the thought of an eviction notice being put on my door before I had the chance to find a new apartment, but then I found one. Just in the nick of time (or so I thought) I finally got approved for an apartment.

The morning of Friday October 24, 2008 was the date I choose to move but when the day finally arrived it rained cats and dogs. So after I dropped my daughter off at school just as I had done every morning before I decided to postpone the move until Saturday and took care of some light errands with the intent of returning to the apartment to complete the last part of what needed to be packed.

I called my cousin and father to inform them that I rescheduled the move for the next day and went to get the lights connected at the new place but I found out I had a past due bill from the year 2000. "When you think you have gotten away with something all it does is come back at an inopportune time and bites you in the bottom." I went to the previous complex but hit a dead end, after I completed that task I picked up my mom who volunteered me to pick up my sister's friend and take her to the airport but before I did that I went to the credit union to try and get some money but was not able to.

As you can see, when my priority should have been packing, I was out running all kinds of errands instead. When I finally got home at six thirty pm I was exhausted, tired, and just wanted to go to sleep. Yes, I was on the verge of eviction, but as long as I still lived there it was home. As I tried to turn the key in the lock I was shocked to discover that it would not budge… "Oh No!" I thought, "the leasing office has changed the lock and locked all me and Niyla's stuff in the house."

Full of dread, brutally my heart hammered against my chest as I wondered, "what am I going to do?" Meanwhile my boyfriend pulled up asked what's going on and at that moment I broke down and told him the whole truth. I never made him aware of how I was drowning in bills, behind on everything, and on the brink of collapse. Unsurprisingly he was furious, but I thought what right did he have to be angry?

Yes, he did have some knickknacks in the apartment, but what I had was priceless things that could never be replaced.

Sure I had mislead him about the severity of my situation but I never thought it would go this far! In the mist of my panic and mild anger I made the decision to take my daughter to my mother's and I went to my boyfriend's house (since he did not live far from the place I was locked out of) but I could scarcely sleep a wink.

The next morning I left his house at around 6am for I was on my way to Cottage at Hampton's leasing office with every intention of sitting outside until it opened. However, since it was early I went to Wal-Mart bought some cleaning supplies for my new place, then went to the complex and waited. But boy did I have a long wait ahead of me because the office did not open until ten am and it was just eight am. Finally when ten o'clock arrive so did the manager of the complex.

I gave her a second to settle, and then I went inside filled with nervous energy and asked if she could unlock the apartment door so that I could get my things. She replied cheerfully, *"Oh your things are gone."* I said *"what do you mean my things are gone?"* *"Well,"* she said *"we evicted you; your things were on the curb. What people did not take we threw away."* What! My heartfelt like it stopped, I was devastated. I then said to her, *"but everything I have and am was in there."* In response, she smiled and said *"that's what happens when you don't pay your rent."*

It was like a slap, no a punch to my stomach because I could barely breath, I could not believe it. I refused to believe it. There I was amazed, frightened, and overcome with pain and shock because not one trace of my things did I see anywhere the day before on the curb. Numb with pain at the magnitude of my loss I decided to go back to the apartment (but could not help but think …since when does a person get evicted and the gate and mailbox key still work…)and ask the neighbor who lived next door if she saw anyone's personal effects in the breezeway, but she did not so I called 911. I really felt that all my things were locked in the apartment.

Let's face it most of us have all seen how it looks after someone has been evicted, and it did not look like that.

On the line with the 911 operator, I informed her that I was evicted yet lied when I told her my daughter's medicine was locked in the apartment and the manager would not let me into the apartment. The purpose of the lie was to get the door opened to ensure that all my things were not still in there. So, she sent an officer to the site and for those few moments I had hope. When the officer arrived, he went into the office, spoke to the manager, came out, and told me *"Oh your things are gone, I spoke to the lady and she said your things are gone..."*

Was everything really gone? I was never even given the opportunity to retrieve any of my things. I wanted to scream why me Lord? But I already knew why. I was reaping what I sowed and rarely do we think the crime justifies the punishment. Fear, disbelief, pain, and anxiety gripped me, words escaped me, and doom overtook me.

With the manager's cold smile and statement *"that's what happens when you don't pay your rent"* echoing through my head, despite the pain I tried to figure out how I would put back the scattered pieces of my broken life but then at that moment I wondered, "Why is it constantly happening to me?" Do I really want those scattered pieces back in place?"

At the age of 27 I expected myself to have already gotten married, to be making over six figures, and have owned a beautiful house, even though I had no clear path or plan of how to make that happen.
Unfortunately the reality was that I was 27 years old with bad credit, a dead end job, and lived in what many (myself included) would consider the ghetto. Just thinking about the money I made and all the bills I had to pay left me wondering; how would I make it and who could help me?

"Who can I run too?" I wondered that constantly. When I needed money, who could I run too? When I needed gas, who could I run too? When I needed food, bills paid, and clothes for my daughter I wondered who could I run too? Who could help me who would help me? I was in a terrible state of mind barely coping but always wondering "who can I run too?" The answer was simple no one for everyone else was trying to help themselves or whining because no one else was.

Struggle had become my first and last name and up to that point I allowed myself to be satisfied with need and lack. Change was forced upon me. No longer did I have the luxury of feeling sorry for myself, no longer would I cry out at night wondering who and why no one was helping me. For God was and is my provider, He created all and owns all. So because he is my father I need only step into my inheritance and receive what he has for me. I would stop looking back at my constant fall from grace. I desired to move forward, to rise out of mediocrity to victory, financial freedom, security, and trust for my success begins with me. Was it really that simple?

PONDERING MY GROWTH

1). Have you had a why me...i.e. adverse life changing moment?

_____
_____
_____

2.) In reliving that past adverse life changing event for those brief moments how did it make you feel?

_____
_____
_____

3.) Have you forgiven yourself or the individual you feel was at fault?

_____
_____
_____

4.) Are you running form something? If so, can you continue to run from it when it is the very thing stopping you from moving forward?

_____
_____
_____

Journaling My Thoughts
Notes from the Book

Chapter 2

PICKING UP THE PIECES

"I keep going because I know there is much more to me than the girl that always needs the hand out..."

So, there I was broken, evicted from a second apartment, left with nothing but the clothes on me and my daughter's back, my car, and whatever else was in there. In the natural, it seemed as if I had nothing left. Let's be honest I felt like nothing. Nothing! Repeat it with me ...Nothing! I just wanted to give up and accept my defeat. I wanted to accept what appeared to be my lot in life, it was as if I was meant to struggle but I could not give up, if not for my own sake at least for my daughter's.

Yes I have a little one and she was my little super trooper, she never complained, trusted my decisions no matter how bad they were, believed in me and had an unwavering faith in my ability as only a child could. Also, I was given an olive branch in the form of the apartment I was able to get right before I was evicted, even if at times it did not seem as such. Determined to do right by this place I had to pick up the pieces, but guess what, to say it was much easier than doing it especially when all I seemed to do was fail.

I knew that my mishaps in life were a direct result of my lack of discipline and drive to follow through with anything. I had to do something new (but it is not easy detraining oneself). However it was a necessary task for my success. How could I pick up the pieces of my life? After much contemplation I realized that I had to change my habits and mindset. Quickly I identified the three main things that affected me the most adversely;

1. I lived my life through the social media and in some ways still do. In other words every night I went home, plopped on the bed, and watched television or got on the computer to see what celebrity was doing what, instead of working on getting out of my dead end job mentioned in chapter one. Some might wonder, could the social media really be that bad? As it related to me yes it was because I lacked control. Social entertainment became a form of containment and distraction.

I realized that I was living through the imitations of lives portrayed on the television, not realizing that those actors were living their dream while I watched from the sideline always wishing I had what they have but doing nothing to make it happen. It got so bad I would gossip about the lives of those celebrities like I knew them. Do not get me wrong, the Lord and everybody else knew how much I loved to watch television. How was I ever going to break that crippling habit?

Since childhood one of the few joys I had outside of eating (that's another story) was television. I could live my life through a movie for it represented freedom, when I watched television I could imagine it was me enjoying a wonderful life, versus living the reality of not having food, a bed, and the basic necessities that others around me had that my parents could not afford. Television, social media, and food became my cloak of comfort.

2. My insecurities with myself took over; I never thought I was good enough nor had enough to offer anyone. I considered myself a failure and wondered on more occasions than one how anyone could love me. I thought I had nothing worthy to offer. Once I got a boyfriend my insecurities caused me to have an unrealistic and unhealthy dependence on him. My life revolved around him, not by his doing but my own. Constantly I sought his approval. Was I too fat? Was I pretty enough? Do you really love me? On and on I went. Without me realizing it, I had romanticized relationships under the mistaken assumption that the end result would be a fairytale, "Happily Ever After" thanks to television and all those romance novels I read.

What is ironic is for years I was extremely lonely all I thought I wanted was a man and once I got one, everything would be peaches and cream. Boy did I get a reality check! For sometimes your growth as a person and pursuit of success takes a back seat to the matters of the heart. There I was finally in a relationship, yet still a part of me was empty and unsatisfied. I felt like something was missing and broken and my boy friend and I suffered for It because I tried to fulfill the void through him.

At times I thought the void in my life was caused by money because realistically speaking, it would be great to have an abundance of it and not worry about how I would pay all bills due, provide food, and shelter. But that could not be the root of it or so many of the wealthy would not be so unhappy, because money with no Christ In your life is fickle and fleeting and whatever joy you are able to obtain will not last. And goodness knows that my joy was fickle and very fleeting.

3. The lack of Christ in my life, I did not make God my priority. When times were hard I ran to the Lord by way of the church but as soon as things began to look up I stopped doing everything and returned to my bad habits. "Yep, Houston, we had a backslider" constantly I went back and forth never staying constant. I did yearn for a real relationship with God but I was doing a terrible job of making it happen. This caused me to question if I really ever trusted God. Did I really believe he could do what he said he would do in the Bible?

Whatever it was, I had to change something quick. The clock was ticking and I was not entirely certain that it was moving in my favor.

- ✓ **Unhealthy attachment to the social media**
- ✓ **Self- Hate; Insecurities**
- ✓ **Godless; Lack of Christ in my life**

Now that I identified the three main things that hindered my growth the most I should have been able to do was move forward with a plan of attack (Operation get my life together) but goodness it was hard starting from scratch. Especially with the weight of pass failures and losses constantly lurking in my shadow. The negative reminders of my pass bore me down to no avail.

To say you have nothing is an understatement until you truly have nothing. It took me losing all my earthly possessions for me to realize that I should not define myself by the material belongings I have but by my character. With this long overdue revelation I started working towards that change, but not just the change of my actions but also my mindset and thought patterns. I had stored years and years of wrong thinking that needed to be reversed. But how? I thought that by having a vision for my life and forcefully working hard to obtain it would help to end the constant hardship.

The problem with that solution was I had no clear path of what my vision, goals, and purpose for life was. All I knew was that I yearned to rid my life of the lack, debt, and hardship that I had known for so long, and not just face, but conquer the fear I had for the unknown. I hoped it would not be too difficult considering this whole approach was foreign to me. For so long (even in those moments) I wanted the benefits of success but with none of the work it required to obtain it.

How could I initiate change while piecing my life back together when already I was back to my bad habits? Already I was late on my car note, the rent was past due, and I did not even want to think about my daughter's after school, plus I was behind on not one but two insurance payments, and the electric bill was past due. Did I mention my daughter and I were in need of food and clothes! I needed so much but my check would hardly cover half of the things listed. So I continued to fall behind digging a new ditch. Was there any hope for me? Would I lose my way, again?

PONDERING MY GROWTH

What did you do after that adverse life changing event to pick up the pieces of your life?

_____
_____
_____
_____

Was rebuilding easy or difficult?

_____
_____
_____
_____

What are some ways that you can improve your life? Whether it is physically, spiritually, or financially.

_____
_____
_____
_____

Journaling My Thoughts
Notes from the Book

Chapter 3

WILL THIS DEFINE ME?

"Never allow the adversity in life define you, for in those moments of hardship lies the catalyst to your destiny..."

Debt, lack, struggle, failure, and can't were all words that defined me, my existence, and my past lot in life. But I began to ask myself, "Is this what I want to be known by?" Am I doomed to struggle for the rest of my life? Would I always have more bills than money? I felt like the deadbeat who had nothing to offer anyone. I have lived in nine apartments, owned two cars, defaulted on most of my bills, and made one bad decision after another. When would I finally break the cycle? Was there not more to me than being the one that always needed the hand out?

More often than not I felt like my life was on repeat, rewind and let's do it again? Why did I constantly go without when there was so much opportunity surrounding me? God gave me hope and a desire for more but, how would I ever obtain it? Doing without had been a part of my life for so long that I did not know how it felt to live otherwise. On the outside looking in at the various people I thought would have nothing (...i.e. judged) it appeared that they now had great jobs, better benefits, nice cars, homes, and traveled often. But, there I was a year and a half later at 29 years old still trying to make something of the sort happen.

At times the weight of my responsibilities weighed me down. This caused me to feel like I had no one to go to for help. I would wonder if God even heard me. Did he care that for the first time ever I was consistently paying almost all bills on time? I successfully carried car insurance for a year, which I never done before. For once I was walking in integrity and going to church. I was changing, did that not count for anything.

Was he ever going to increase my territory? In church the pastor said "seek God first and there is no way you can't be blessed" I tried to do that but, yet I continued to find myself thinking about all the things I was in need of and constantly contemplated to myself if I would ever overcome? If I allowed my circumstance of lack to define me, I would be doomed to live in poverty for the rest of my life always hoping for someone's provision.

At that point I was drained and lost. In all the years of my life, I do not believe that I had ever been as drained or distraught emotionally. I did not know where I would go from there. I always had a path or a direction, though I did not always follow through with it there was always another plan. Frankly my life was in shambles. I could have gone deeper into the bottomless abyss of my sorrows indefinitely, but I did not. After all there were my dreams and aspirations for myself and my daughter to consider.

It became a necessity for me to encourage myself. But how could I encourage myself when I felt lower than the dirt, I was empty with nothing positive left to uplift myself. Just looking over my life would bring tears to my eyes. Thinking about the loss of all I held dear grieved me, the baby pictures of my daughter, and all the priceless things were gone forever. For days the bitter taste of failure made it difficult to cope. But, (I thank God for a… but) the Lord said "weeping may endure for a night but joy comes in the morning". When would my morning get here?

Trying desperately to identify the positive, my mind could only identify my inadequacies. Filled with worry, doubt, and fear at the possibility that this was my life and all I was to expect from it. The life of my parents was a constant struggle and I feared that such a fate was also my lot in life. To never have enough, to work hard every day yet have nothing to show for it, and to never have the opportunity to live and enjoy life. Then I was reminded of Luke 1:37 "For with God nothing shall be impossible" simple yet powerful. It was not long before I thought of Ephesians 3:20 "now unto him who is able to do exceedingly abundantly above all I can ask or think according to the power that work in me." The peace of those words surrounded me like a warm fire that felt like home. Was all my suffering and struggle for a purpose? There were times that I felt God had something more something great in store for me. In reading those scriptures my faith and hope in God was renewed.

Deciding to strengthen my faith in God, I made an effort to fellowship with the Lord on a more consistent basis. With my renewed hope for a better life, I focused on putting God first and trusting his will for my life. I was assured that as long as I put God first and trust him anything I desired within His will was possible to obtain according to the power that worked in me.

Have you ever thought about the power that works in you? Does your own lack of faith, fear, and belief in self cause you to limit God from being able to give you what he has already promised? Maybe I have limited God. But how did I not allow that mediocrity, complacency, and containment continue to define me?

I had already established that I would change my mind set by no longer staying focused on the negative aspects of my past for all old things have passed away and made new. It was time for me to finally move forward and let go of all the hurt and struggle of yesterday and embrace the grace of a new day. With a new day came the opportunity to obtain success and the ability to accomplish something wonderful. God's mercy is new everyday and so should my zeal for life be. If not before I know it a minute could turn into a hour, a hour to a day, a day to a week, a week to a month, and a month to a year with nothing to show for myself but more of the same, with everything I thought I would have and wanted to accomplish never coming to pass.

Forced upon me was the task to overcome and now was the time to combat my negativity. All the negative words that often spewed from my mouth needed to be replaced with words that roused me to good works, not defeat, and loss. After all, life and death are in the power of the tongue" I had what I said I had". At times in my sadness or when I felt defeated I said negative things about my life and those around me. When you feel lower than the dirt it is hard to speak life to any situation and have joy. Somehow I needed to embrace a more positive thought path and most importantly forgive myself.

Last but certainly not least I had the monumental task of no longer considering myself a failure. At times I found myself still fighting the same battle. I struggled with finding my path in life, being a proper steward of my finances, self esteem, and all the insecurities that went with it. I had to be determined not to allow those faults to define me. I had to believe in myself and in the hope that one day I would live debt free with no sorrow added to it. I wanted joy even in times of trouble, peace in hours of duress, love when I felt loveless, and faith when the journey ahead seemed hopeless. So I was determined to trust the Lord with all my heart and lean not to my own understanding.

Of course, my view was hazy at times, more often than I wanted to admit. With bills to pay, a child to feed, and a life to rebuild at times the pressure of it all seemed unbearable. During those type of moments I took out the couch (which was the word of God) and encouraged myself for I knew that he would never leave me or abandon me. I could not allow myself to be discouraged or distracted by the things of this world but continued to stand. And when I felt like I was about to break down from doubt, lack, and loneliness, I would stand some more until my breakthrough came to pass.

If I did not give up, every vision and dream God planted in me would come to fruition plus more. Thank goodness God is not a respecter of persons; which to me meant that if he brought David from a pasture to a throne he could increase my territory, and if he took Joseph from a pit to head man in Egypt second only to pharaoh, than he could make me fruitful in the place of my affliction. And if he could bless Esther and Ruth with a great man to marry surely he would do the same for me. Everyday my mind strengthened. Where there once was no hope, I now had a minuscule of it. When before all I could feel was defeat, I started to notice small victories.

PONDERING MY GROWTH

Have you allow the adverse life changing event of your pass determine the direction you did or would take in life?

_____
_____
_____
_____

If so was it a positive change or more of the same?

_____
_____
_____
_____

What are some ways that you can improve your life? Whether it is physical, spiritual, or financial.

_____
_____
_____
_____

Journaling My Thoughts
Notes from the Book

_____
_____
_____
_____
_____
_____
_____
_____
_____
_____
_____
_____
_____
_____
_____
_____
_____
_____
_____

Chapter 4

HOW I OVERCAME

"Out of the Ashes of My Suffering came the Strength to obtain Victory"

After years of battling against the downward spiral of my own inadequacies, I finally came to the point where I made the choice to change. The obstacle I encountered was how to advance my plan of change to action. At a crossroad with no clear direction on how to obtain the success I so yearned for, I wondered what I could do? For years I looked at others' success and never thought to take the steps to have my own. Well, that is not entirely true I have had several ideas, from owning a restaurant, producing a documentary, creating a courier service, to -worst of all- living my dreams through my daughter.

However two constants always stopped me, laziness, and fear. The laziness was self explanatory. I wanted all the results and none of the sweat equity. As for the fear that was I different story. I had a fear of failure, fear of what people thought of me; and a fear of stepping outside of my very small comfort zone. Why I allowed fear to have such a strong hold on me I do not know. Perhaps it was because I was too blind to notice how "the fear" had become a stronghold that thwarted my growth. Once I was told that fear was "false evidence appearing real." I needed to stop allowing fear to stop me from moving forward with my dreams.

Of course I was still at the dead-end job and what is worse was biannually there was a constant threat of layoff. As far as I was concerned no job was secure, so I had the notion that for me to be successful I needed to take Nike's motto to heart and "just do it." I needed to walk through the fear, step out on faith and seize what God had for me since no one was going to just hand it to me. But what could I do? What was I good at? Let's see; there was cooking talking, reading. All those I thought were useless what could I do with any of that. Than I thought what do I like to do? That was easy watch movies, read books and success stories, cook, talk, help people, oh and cuddling. I pondered that for a while, when what seemed out of nowhere, I had it! What about a book? Could I really write a book?

If a celebrity could do it without even relating to the everyday struggle of the common man, why couldn't I? But as quickly as the thought came, so did my doubts. Who was I kidding I could not write a book! Who would read let alone buy it? Did I not need to first have something interesting to say and be successful? Though I thought I had something to say, one day hoped to be successful, and help anyone in need, while making my mark. I had no clue where to start. So back to the drawing board I went trying to find my niche with a focus on… Success!

* * * * * *

How does one become successful or obtain success? Saying I need to achieve success was one thing, but carrying it out was another thing. After all, how would I define my own success? Webster defines it as, "the attainment of wealth, favor, or eminence." "Wow" I thought, I want that! Having wealth would be wonderful, but I would not ever have it by being an employee. My solution, Become the employer! But there was still a problem. Entrepreneurs simply found ways to profit from new and innovative ideas. What would mine be?

With little, rather no money for major start up cost and a residing awareness that my talents centered on nothing in particular, I seemed to be left with nothing. Now I had a new dilemma I finally had the will to make something happen but lacked any rational business ideas that did not take major startup cost. So for the next few days I racked my brain. Eventually days became weeks then weeks became months when finally I had an idea.

It has always been a desire of mine to own a restaurant, but of course I never tried. I knew I could never obtain the financing due to laziness and my lack of desire to create a business plan, not to mention that I had bad credit. Then I thought," what if I started a catering business, not just any catering business, but one that provided the missing side or dish for any occasion." It would be perfect! I could do it from home and it had relatively low startup cost. And just like that "SouthernSides" was born. Our motto was "We make time, so you can too." Almost every step of trying to build SouthernSides I was afraid Constantly I wondered what others would think of me but I pushed through my fear and did it afraid but willingly. After about two months of trying to get my business off the ground I gave up due to the following issues.

1. I could not get a business license because I cooked in the same kitchen I used personally
2. Working a fulltime job while building a business from scratch totally burned me out, now I did not want to cook point blank period.
3. I realized if I could not do it the right way then I did not want to do it at all.

So back to the drawing board I went wondering what I could do to make money when lo and behold I received a Rich

Dad, Poor Dad flier in the mail (let me put out there when you are desperate for something more you fall for anything). I signed up for the free seminar (who out there know that nothing is free). On July 27, 2009 I attended the free seminar. The speaker was second-rate at best, but what she excelled at was conveying her rags to riches story which somehow struck a chord in me. Why? Perhaps it is because I can only relate to someone who has a similar background as me.

Caught like a fish to a hook, I chose to take the extended three day course that cost $495.00. This was major for me because I could do a lot with that money, but I was assured that I would come out of the extended course equipped with the knowledge needed on how to make at least three thousand dollars in revenue. Hey, I thought it would be an investment into my future. One lesson I learned hard was, to get something out of life you have to put something into it, so I took the leap.

However in pure ironic fashion, three days after I paid for the extended class, I read an article that stated it was a scam. "Lord NO!!" I screamed to myself as fear gripped me, what was I going to do? That is when it hit me. Why stress over something I could not control? I already paid the money and on August 14 through 16, 2009 I would make the best of it and trust God.

I attended the courses. The three days were packed with information. Though I did learn some valuable information, I would not have spent almost five hundred dollars to hear it. Unsurprisingly it was an up-sale, so I hit another dud. Gosh, I could hear that clock ticking again. It felt like old age, dreams never discovered, and a race against time. Lord knows I was tired of being broke, telling my daughter not today, and barely making it! And, to add insult to injury, no one really took me seriously. All people thought I did was talk. Sure I was a dreamer and on occasion shared my hopes and ambitions with others; just because it did not happen within a timely manner did that make me any less of a source. Most of my family even my boyfriend sought business counsel elsewhere anywhere but with me. They would one day see that I would be a success.

How to make money? How to make money was the million dollar question. I tell you if desperation had a 'stench' it would be a number one seller called "Ahlumba!" September 5th, 2009, I decided to take a break from thinking about money and that was when it happened. While cleaning up my closet an idea I had earlier in the week came back to me 'OneMansJunk.'

You see I had a lot of clothes that was given to me that I never wore because they could not fit or simply not my style. Originally, I was going to throw them all away because my old friend "lazy" came to visit and I did not feel like taking it all to Goodwill. I was tired of seeing all that in my closet. But after observing how many pieces I had, I knew it would be wrong to throw the clothes away when so many go without. So out of my need I decided to fulfill someone else's. By providing new and used household items to families in need regardless of race, gender, ethnicity, and/or religion at no cost to the individual. Yes, with this idea firm in mind I decided to start a nonprofit organization. Go ahead…queue the horror music…That meant more money.

One year later…going down the road of making this nonprofit a reality I was met with extreme difficulties. Money is what seemed to make the world go around and without it the process was long and tedious. Already I had invested an excess of sweat equity and over $1550.00! This dream was draining me dry! February 2010, I paid 149.00 for registered agent, 150.00 for articles of incorporation, about 50.00 for the domain, 60.00 for the P.O.Box. and in September 2010, I acquired…i.e. hired the services of a foundation group to handle the legalization (501c3 Status) of the nonprofit which was costing me 170.00 plus interest a month because I could not afford to pay the 1500.00 straight out.

When February 2011 arrived and finally the 501c3 application was completed the joy I felt in that moment was unparallel. Finally it was coming together. But, (there is always a 'but') who knew the IRS charged 850.00 to process the application. "What the?!" Could a word be a question and a scream? Please tell me, where was I going to get 850.00 from? I was already strapped for cash, so once again the worry and fear stepped in and those seedy words that lingered in the back of my mind popped in my head and sang it's little song "I can't…I can't do this" and at that moment I was forced to make a decision. Would I maintain a purpose in spite of difficulty?

I made the decision to push onward. To produce the extra money needed for the nonprofit, I decided to begin a for-profit business. But alas that took me back to the drawing board. Now down and discouraged at the prospect of what I spent so much time trying to make come to fruition, now felt as if it was no more. I had hit a brick wall- the brick wall of no money, for without it I could go no further with OneMansJunk. But I had to go further with the nonprofit; it represented one of the things I held deep to my heart. I wanted to be able to provide an outlet that helped the working poor for real. For there were many times when I needed help but because I was actively trying to better myself the only way I could obtain aid was if I lied.

I would not give up! God has instilled greatness in us all (though many fail to live up to their potential). I knew that greatness was in me and I was determined to see what I felt on the inside be evident on the outside. I just needed to find my niche. I would not give up. I often sat and imagined life with nothing wanted or needed, to never be late on one bill, to live debt free, and never have to say "one day." But just like all fantasies it appeared to be a fleeting figment that was unattainable.

I know I should look to the hill whence cometh my help; for my help cometh from the lord. When would my help get here and stay? I was really trying to stay the path and in faith while working towards that goal of making OMJ a reality. But everyday it was something different. The price of food was through the roof, gas was through the roof, my goodness cost of living period was through the roof but inconveniently the only thing below average was my wages.

I knew the Lord said he would not put more on me than I could bear and that he would never leave me nor forsake me. But, it was hard to stay positive when my stomach was empty. I could barely afford miscellaneous things I needed and worst of all I had to choose between paying a bill or have money in my pocket…it was basically a lose- lose situation.

Many days I felt like my life was on repeat; where I got paid just to go through the same cycle of lack, struggle, want, and need again, again, again, and again. So how would I reach my dream of entrepreneurship when I did not even know where to start anymore? And once again I began to hear that worrisome ticking and was overtaken by the feeling that my life was a race and I was lagging far behind while time was steadily moving against me. Yet everyone else was halfway through or crossing the finish line of success.

It became hard to stay focused but I took comfort in the old saying that it is the slow and steady that endure and overcome not the quick and the fast. Still, I stressed over how I could continue to keep the faith when I saw no end in sight. Every so often I felt lost and wanted someone to talk to… to help sort out my path but realized there was no couch waiting for me to lie on and no one to talk to. It was in those moments that I had to trust my heavenly father, encourage myself and keep the faith that there was no way He brought me through all the former hardship of my pass just to leave me upstream without a paddle.

Whenever I was feeling defeated, another thing that helped keep me going besides my faith in the Lord was my extreme borderline unhealthy love for success stories. It was and still is nice to know that someone accomplished a dream that otherwise seemed impossible. I rejoiced in anyone's success because I knew if God did it for them he could do it for me. Those success stories inspired me to keep going like gas from a gas station - I could run until my next fill up.

One day I was having one of those days when I needed some extra encouragement, so I watched Jennifer Hudson's behind the music and I have to say, "her story is amazing!" It totally inspired me, because she persevered when odds were stacked against her. She pushed even when there were times she possibly did not know what she was pushing for. She had faith not just in herself but in God knowing that even if a door was closed and it seemed like there was no other option, God would provided another. It made me think about Ephesians 3:20 again which says " now unto him who is able to do exceedingly abundantly above all you can ask or think according to the power that works in you"

I asked the question again of myself; what power did I have in me? Was I still hindering God by my very words, actions, and thoughts? So after all that it seemed that I was back to the original question; would I maintain a purpose in spite of difficulty? Yes! Though I was up to my neck in obscurity, I would maintain my purpose in spite of difficulty. I would endure. So to the drawing board I went (I was starting to feel like the energizer battery) but this time the idea was not so long in the making. This time I had a plan. What I did was write down things that interested me, something I would do for free and the two constants' that I found were, that I loved real stories of success that inspire and helping those in need. After three days of brainstorming, "Inspired2prosper" was born.

Inspired2prosper was a way for me to provide hope to the hopeless. Just as I was once hopeless and lost, I wanted anyone who yearned for something more (but because of their circumstances thought it was impossible) to know that no matter how low it seems you have fallen as long as you have a desire and a will almost anything was possible. I became an advocate for what I called "the hopeless." I wanted to help people realize their dreams. I wanted them to see if I could change my circumstance anyone could.

So, I created a website that would be a one stop shop for anyone who needed to be encouraged, uplifted and inspired. For so long I was lost, so it felt good to have a focus and purpose. To sum it up Inspired2prosper's main purpose was (and still is) to motivate and uplift anyone who has lost hope or was in need of encouragement by way of the internet, books, social media, inspirational speaking, paraphernalia, ect....

Success is all around us, not just what is depicted on television. For that reason my focus is not success based on the amount of wealth obtained, but victory in every aspect of life. I had to learn that no accomplishment was too small. My accomplishments started small but grew in magnitude as time went on. But of course while I was going through, it was extremely hard for me to see anything I did as good.

I went from never having car insurance too consistently, I went from never paying a bill to not paying one late in almost three years. I went from being a very insecure girl and over 60 pounds overweight to becoming a confident young lady who was featured in the Atlanta Journal Constitution health and wellness section online and in print. I went from thinking that, me ever having the opportunity to appear on television was nothing but a pipe dream to being given the opportunity to be interviewed for a weight loss show "The Weigh We Were" to aired on one of my most favorite broadcast network from childhood. And of course I found my entrepreneurial niche by doing something I never realized that I loved but brought out through my journey 'writing.'

Who would have ever thought that I who dropped out of high school with the biggest fear of writing would ever write a book? I did, but only in dreams that I thought was unattainable. I accomplished what I thought was impossible, obtained what I thought was unattainable, and achieved what I thought was unachievable. Finally I had a clear path, finally I had a goal, finally I knew my vision and the course was no longer set or focused on selfish gain.

It is not the ideal for many people for I have been asked several times how would I make money and for once I could say money was not forefront on my mind for this is a labor of love and once you find your passion the money will always eventually come. Finally I would put this mouth to good use versus being the bearer of misery.

For years I searched for a way to enrich my life and received nothing but more of the same. It was not until I made the decision to stop the negative self destructive cycle of my actions that positive change began to take root in my life. I began to have The Field of Dreams mindset "if I build it, they will come." Though times were hard I knew that if I did not give up and stay the course, I would eventually have my success.

Never could or would I have imagined that there would ever come a time that I appreciate the pain and suffering of my pass for out of it was my salvation. I could do it all along I just had to believe in myself, trust God, and not be so dependent on others, for when people get tired and leave you God never will. He is just waiting for you to step out on faith trust him and do it so he can show up and show out. Never forget to persevere, persevere, persevere, and persevere some more. Webster defines success as the attainment of wealth, favor, or eminence and with confidence I declare that I am well on my way. Now my journey begins...

PONDERING MY GROWTH

How did you overcome your adverse life changing event?

_____
_____
_____

If not how do you plan to overcome?

_____
_____
_____

Will you maintain purpose inspire of difficulty?

_____
_____
_____

What are some ways that you can improve your life? Whether it be physical, spiritual, or financial.

_____
_____
_____

Journaling My Thoughts
Notes from the Book

Chapter 5

YOU CAN TOO!

"Do not say what you would have done, if you never did"

My childhood and adult life up to this point was a disparity, always lacking. Constantly I wished for more, but wishing was not enough. Dreaming and hoping was half the battle. The other half was about taking action, having persistence, consistency, diligence, and just pure hard work. It is a will and determination to stay the path no matter what adversity may come your way, a resolve to never lose hope that you can and will see your faith through to the end.

One of my favorite scriptures in the bible comes from Romans 4:18 which states "who against hope believed in hope". When all the evidence before you points to defeat and the impossibility to accomplish a feat, that is when you girt yourself with the word of God and remember your hope. We all should expect the best even though we have every reason to believe the worst.

In my journey to prosper in every area of my life, I

encountered many mishaps, disappointments, and doubts, but I pushed through those road blocks even though there were moments when I believed it would be much easier to give up, let go of ambition and settle with a life of just enough. But, the Lord constantly would bring me in remembrance of my hopes, dreams, visions, and goals for my future. He also taught me patience; I was one of the most impatient individuals out there. I had no tolerance and craved instant gratification. I was not aware that the lord needed to take me through a season of development for he knew that not only was I not ready, but I also could not be trusted with the magnitude of increase he had in store for me. After all where much is given, much is required.

Most have seen and admired the beauty of a natural pearl, but its splendor does not come about without some sort of annoyance to its carrier. There is a process of development that comes at a price to producing such a thing of worth. A clam is irritated by a speck of sand and as a defense mechanism it creates a fluid to rid or protect itself from the intrusion but to no avail. All along, layer upon layer of this fluid is deposited over the speck of sand until a beautiful pearl is formed.

Often we look at the struggles that come against us as a fate worse than... Not realizing that sometimes we have to go through the process of pain to produce the end result of greatness! Of course, any success we hope to obtain will not come with ease, without sacrifice or possible discomfort.

During my development stage there were many times when my faith, trust, and hope were tested. At times, it seemed to the very limit. Constantly, I felt like I was being built up just to be violently let down in the end. But I thank God that my steps were ordered by him, that he had a purpose for me. So it did not matter how many times I fell -as long as I got back up, because he never let me go. I am a living witness that all things are possible to those who will not just believe but continue to believe. I have had opportunities open up for me that in the natural seemed impossible and only attainable or imagined in a dream, to achieve. So do not ever receive the negative saying "only in your dreams" because if you can dream it and it is in God's will then you surely can achieve it. Why not dream big?

* * * * * *

Think back to when you were younger and unafraid to dream. Did you ever with all certainty say things such as "I'm going to do this, be that, make at least this" or "I will never gain that much weight, let him or her do that to me…" Fast forward 10-15 years, what happened to your dream? What happened to your ambition? What happened to your boldness? Somehow your hope was lost and can't, should, would, and could of took over.

I have garnered encouragement from diverse areas and one thing is for certain, scarcity, and fear has no prejudice. It does not matter who you are where you have been, or what you have gone through, there is always opportunity available for you to change your tomorrow by doing something different today. Granted, some might have to work harder than others but we all have our own path to travel down. So today why not put aside that false evidence appearing real, dare to dream and declare your success.

Below I introduce the nine key principals that really helped me to achieve positive change. I hope that it will assist in giving you that extra push you might need to keep going.

9 Key Principles to Achieve Positive Change in Your Life:

1. Have a Dream, Vision, or Goal
2. Faith, Believe that your Dream is Possible
3. Action, Work towards making the Dream a Reality
4. Endure with Patience, No Success comes easy or without some Sacrifice
5. Declare it, Be unafraid & comfortable with speaking it aloud
6. Envision, Meditate on where you will be, not where you are
7. Prayer, Go before the Lord Daily & he will renew your Strength
8. Not Impossible, But easier said than done
9. **Persist, keep trying, Never give up & it shall come to Pass**

Have faith in God for if I would have been told almost three years ago (or any years ago) that I would be featured in a mainstream news paper, interviewed on television, a entrepreneur, and now author it would have been difficult to believe. I would have said "shut your mouth, such things are only possible in my dreams". But, not only have I achieved these things, I also surpassed my own expectations, and for that reason I not only give thanks to Jesus Christ my Lord and Savior but to all the others before me who's journeys of success has and still is Inspiring me to Prosper. My mission to you is to be Inspired2prosper and if you so choose to accept your journey can also begin.

Begin your Journey

Now is the time to be active in making your dream a reality. Why not start today! Remember the 9 steps of change Dare to Dream Big and Declare your Success. I know if you have this book then you too are Inspired2prosper.

Begin your Journey:

What is your dream, vision, or goal for yourself or future? Whatever it may be do not be ashamed of the magnitude or the minuteness of it.

_____

_____

_____

Do you believe your dream, vision, or goal is attainable? Why or why not?

_____

_____

_____

What actions are you taking to make your dream a reality?

_____

_____

_____

As the time pass and your dream, vision, or goal has not come to fruition; what do you do to stay patient and encouraged?

_____
_____
_____

Do you daily declare your, dream, vision, or goal for your future…i.e. speak those things that be not as though they were?

_____
_____
_____

Are you a talker or a doer? If a doer why are you allowing another day pass without truly pursuing your dream, vision, or goal?

_____
_____
_____

INSPIRED2PROSPER

Journaling My Thoughts
How I Plan to Begin My Journey...

AUTHOR'S AFTERTHOUGHT

I wrote this book while I was going through an extremely trying time in my life. I choose to write it that way so that you, the reader could know the true extent of my pain and struggle as it happened. Though I focused on my financial difficulties, there were many other battles with which I struggled. Everything from my relationship with the Lord, my weight, my low self-esteem , the hardship of being a good mother, to finding myself, fighting homelessness, and battling the pain from being repeatedly cheated on has been a struggle.

Times were not always easy. Actually, it was downright painful, but I thank God for faith to believe in something more and hope. Though, at times it felt like I was in a time warp saying and experiencing the same negative things over and over again while my circumstance dictated loss, no money, no home, and failure at every end. The Lord allowed me to feel and see something more in myself. He gave me a dream, a desire to believe in something more.

According to Philemon 1:6 "The release of my faith will produce the existence of every good thing which is in me in Christ Jesus". I interpreted that as meaning I already had the ability in me all along to own my own business, diner, be a inspirational speaker, NY Times Best Selling Author, start a Non-Profit to help anyone in need, and own my own home. I just had to release my faith, put forth the work to make it happen, and believe. At times it was hard to come out of my mouth because I was embarrassed by what people would say or think.

There I was with nothing, the lowest one on the totem pole, the girl who always needed the hand out having the nerve to tell somebody "I was going to be something big." I would get the yeah right smile or laugh. That is why it is important that you surround yourself with like minded, uplifting people because sometimes people are unintentional dream killers. I have noticed that negativity is embraced while positivity is laughed at.

Example one is pro-negativity:
If you were to go to work today and say to person A "girl I'm so broke I don't know how I'm going to make it" or " I hate this job" or " you will probably get a response of " Okay, I feel ya", and a high five.

Now let us look at Example 2:
You go to work and person A is complaining and you reply with "I will not receive that, I will speak life into my situation instead of death, I have more money then I know what to do with, my life is wonderful, the Lord is truly blessing me" Person A will not stand there and listen to that long but will leave find somebody else to complain to then begin gossiping about you because they will only see your current circumstance

That is why it is important to choose your counsel wisely. Everyday be bold and thank God for those things that be not as though they were until one by one it truly is. No matter how long it takes or how impossible it may seem, never give up on a God given dream. Keep in mind that success and prosperity is not just evident through financial wealth but also through the accomplishment of being able to overcome any hindering obstacle in your life by making a positive change. In conclusion I share a hard lesson learned; in life there is no Happily Ever After but there is a "I will be happy while I go through my after" and in everything give thanks.

SOMETHING EXTRA

In the nearly three years ago that I hit rock bottom I began a hobby. "Journaling!" It was a great way for me to release all the painful thoughts, hurt, fear, and loneliness of my plight. Many nights I would take out my pink notebook that at one point began to represent failure and write. While writing, that not only was a time of release but priceless moments of fellowship with the Lord. He knew everything about me, I did not have to fake or hide anything, so the Lord became the close friend I always yearned for in a person.

In those moments of release my writings became letters to the Lord about various events in my life some of which I turned into poems (which is ironic because I always disliked poems). So I encourage you to journal for you never know where it might take you. If nothing else it is always great to see where you have been which could help you to know where you are going. Please enjoy

INSPIRED2PROSPER

CHANGE IS ON THE WAY

There are things I want to do
I feel a bubbling on the inside
Have I been given another chance?
My thoughts are everywhere
Yet I try to stay focused
Keep my eye on the prize
Will I ever get out of here?
This dead end job that barely allow ends to meet
After paying about three bills
I'm left with nothing wondering
From one day to the next
What will I get?
Or shall I say come my way
It's hard to stay focused,
Determined, and in faith
I believe God did not give me
This vision, desire, and dream for nothing
But it is up to me to trust and believe
That change is on the way

WHERE HAVE I BEEN

I feel completely empty and lost on the inside
Daily I feel myself drifting further away
Away from my dreams
Away from my faith
Yes, I know what I must do to have more
But lately I don't have the will to make anything happen
Do I really have what it takes?
What it takes to obtain and sustain success
I'm tired, so tired of dreams
Dreams that never seem to become reality
Tired of my job
But have to appreciate it
Tired of wanting to go someplace
Yet have no clue where to go
Tired of that guy calling me sweetie
Yet not speaking it, but letting it go
Tired of smiling when I want to cry
Worst of all
I'm tired of myself
So when I inquire where have I been?
I have been lost without a lasting desire
To find my way back

I AM

There are many things I am not
I am not the prettiest
I am not the most successful
I am not the fittest
But I am and always will be
The only me
Yes! Women are a dime a dozen
I am not
You said you loved me
But that love has yet to be shown
Your words were idle declarations that fell on dead ground
I gifted you my heart
In return you rewarded me with
Lies, betrayal, and promises you never intend to fulfill
What could I do, say, or give to make you love me
But you cannot love someone who does not love
themselves
Now we are no more
But it was evident
We were over before the actual end

BE THANKFUL

I was desperate for something
So I prayed for anything
But once I received it
I found reason to complain
I got what I asked for but now I am in pain
The very thing I thought I wanted has changed

WORTHY

I have to believe I'm beautiful
I have to believe I'm worthy
Because thoughts creep into tell me I'm worthless
At night as the sun sets
So does the loneliness of my heart
And all the hype I fed it
For all I can think about is
Why did he not call?
As one day ends another begins
But my thoughts still bang in my head
Highs and lows, highs and lows
Will you really let your happiness be determined by a phone call?
I am beautiful
I am worthy
I will not despair for his loss is
Another's gain

INSPIRED2PROSPER

SHARE YOUR STORY WITH US

Have you obtained some personal success? Why not share it with us?
Don't worry know success is ever to small to share, we want to celebrate with you...

If you have any questions, concerns, or inspiring words, please feel free to contact us at:
CONTACTUS@INSPIRED2PROSPER.COM

IF YOU WOULD LIKE TO FIND OUT MORE ABOUT INSPIRED2PROSPER:
WWW.AHLUMBA.COM
WWW.INSPIRED2PROSPER.COM

YOU CAN LIKE US ON FACEBOOK:
WWW.FACEBOOK.COM/INSPIRED2PROSPER
WWW.FACEBOOK.COM/AHLUMBAH

FOLLOW US ON TWITTER:
WWW.TWITTER.COM/I2P_INTL

DOWNLOAD OUR FREE APP 'MORNING CUP OF JO' FROM THE GOOGLE PLAY STORE

ABOUT THE AUTHOR

Ahlumba, a high school dropout, a college dropout, and a single mother of one who had the fortitude to search for and obtain more despite the mediocrity of her past that tried to contain her. Just like you she is constantly seeking to improve her physical, spiritual, and financial well being for she is in a journey to reach her destiny.

www.ingramcontent.com/pod-product-compliance
Lightning Source LLC
Chambersburg PA
CBHW032213040426
42449CB00005B/569